Learn to Carve Faces

THE BASIC EAR

ISBN 978-1-56523-581-6 (kit)

ISBN 978-1-56523-624-0 (booklet only)

To learn more about the other great books from Fox Chapel Publishing, or to find a retailer near you, call toll-free 800-457-9112 or visit us at ***www.FoxChapelPublishing.com.***

Note to Authors: We are always looking for talented authors to write new books in our area of woodworking, design, and related crafts. Please send a brief letter describing your idea to Acquisition Editor, 903 Square Street, Mount Joy, PA 17552.

Second Printing
Printed in China

Learn to Carve Faces

THE BASIC EAR

HAROLD ENLOW

FOX CHAPEL
PUBLISHING

Learn to Carve Faces: The Basic Ear

While it's easy to hide an ear behind a lock of hair or under a hat, ears allow you to add a great deal of character to a carving. Ears are simple enough to carve, and like most other features, easy to fix if you make a carving misstep.

On a realistic carving, an ear reinforces the carver's ability to create an image in wood. On a caricature carving, the ears are easy to exaggerate and undersized ears or oversized ears add to the joke of the carving. While you can make the ears oversized, the carving will look better if you carve the same basic structure as a realistic ear.

I have listed what tools I use for this carving, but you can use whatever tools you have on hand—there is no need to use the exact tools I mention as long as you are pleased with the end result.

Basic Ear

Outline the ear. Draw in a rectangle for the ear. Make a stop cut along the top of the rectangle with a carving knife and cut down to the stop cut. Make a stop cut on the bottom of the rectangle and cut up to the stop cut with a carving knife. Make a stop cut on the outside line of the rectangle with a ⅜" #3 gouge and cut up to the stop cut.

Add the notch to the bottom of the ear. Use a carving knife to taper the top outside edge of the ear. Then carve the notch into the side of the ear with a carving knife.

Shape the outside bottom corner of the ear. Round the outside bottom corner of the ear with a carving knife.

Shape the tragus. The tragus is the little flap of skin sticking out of the ear near the face. Stop-cut around the tragus with a carving knife and cut up to the stop cut so the tragus sticks out.

Shape the inside edge of the ear. Carve along the inside edge of the ear with a ⅛" V-tool.

Deepen the area around the tragus. Use a ⅛" V-tool to deepen the area around the tragus. This creates a realistic shadow around the tragus.

Round the edges of the ear. Use a 3⁄16" skew chisel or a carving knife.

Carve the hole in the ear. Make a deep cut with a ⅛" #5 gouge. The hole is positioned just behind the tragus.

Shape the inside of the upper ear. Use a 2mm veiner to carve the Y at the top of the ear. Refine the area and round over the sharp corners with a micro gouge and a detail knife.

Finish shaping the edges of the ear. Use a 3⁄16" skew chisel and a carving knife to refine the overall shape of the ear and to round over any sharp edges.

Undercut the back of the ear. Use a ⅜" #3 gouge to undercut the back of the ear. Refine the back of the ear with a carving knife.

Ear With Hair Over It

16

Lumpy Ear

Ear With Hoop Earing

Round Ear

Elf Ear

Unusual Ear

Carving Faces Workbook

Learn to Carve Facial Expressions with the Legendary Harold Enlow

By Harold Enlow

Follow along with Harold as he teaches you how to carve faces with life and expression.

ISBN: 978-1-56523-585-4

$19.95 • 144 pages

Woodcarving Illustrated Magazine

The How-To Magazine for Carvers

Woodcarving Illustrated delivers the most compelling projects, great photography, and handy tips and techniques for beginning, intermediate, and advanced carvers.

1 year (4 issues) for **$19.95** Subscription rates higher outside the U.S.

Subscribe Today!

www.WoodcarvingIllustrated.com

Notes: